ALL ABOUT INSECTS
ALL ABOUT ANTS

by Karen Latchana Kenney

T0015101

pogo

Ideas for Parents and Teachers

Pogo Books let children practice reading informational text while introducing them to nonfiction features such as headings, labels, sidebars, maps, and diagrams, as well as a table of contents, glossary, and index.

Carefully leveled text with a strong photo match offers early fluent readers the support they need to succeed.

Before Reading

- "Walk" through the book and point out the various nonfiction features. Ask the student what purpose each feature serves.
- Look at the glossary together. Read and discuss the words.

Read the Book

- Have the child read the book independently.
- Invite him or her to list questions that arise from reading.

After Reading

- Discuss the child's questions. Talk about how he or she might find answers to those questions.
- Prompt the child to think more. Ask: Ants live and work together in colonies. Can you name any other insects that work together?

Pogo Books are published by Jump!
5357 Penn Avenue South
Minneapolis, MN 55419
www.jumplibrary.com

Library of Congress Cataloging-in-Publication Data

Names: Kenney, Karen Latchana, author.
Title: All about ants / Karen Latchana Kenney.
Description: Minneapolis, MN: Jump!, Inc., [2024]
Series: All about insects | Includes index.
Audience: Ages 7-10
Identifiers: LCCN 2022043402 (print)
LCCN 2022043403 (ebook)
ISBN 9798885244213 (hardcover)
ISBN 9798885244220 (paperback)
ISBN 9798885244237 (ebook)
Subjects: LCSH: Ants–Juvenile literature.
Classification: LCC QL568.F7 K46 2024 (print)
LCC QL568.F7 (ebook)
DDC 595.79/6–dc23/eng/20220907
LC record available at https://lccn.loc.gov/2022043402
LC ebook record available at https://lccn.loc.gov/2022043403

Editor: Jenna Gleisner
Designer: Emma Almgren-Bersie

Photo Credits: Eric Isselee/Shutterstock, cover, 1; Dreamframer/Shutterstock, 3; Scifier/Shutterstock, 4; Pascal Guay/Shutterstock, 5; Goldi59/iStock, 6-7; blickwinkel/Alamy, 8-9; John Richmond/Alamy, 10-11; Sagar Gore/iStock, 12; Nikita Alexandrov/Dreamstime, 13; Travis Wallace/iStock, 14-15 (top); Deer worawut/Shutterstock, 14-15 (bottom); TT/iStock, 16; Pavel Krasensky/Shutterstock, 17; Khairul Bustomi/Shutterstock, 18-19; Cornel Constantin/Shutterstock, 20-21; Andrey Pavlov/Shutterstock, 23.

Printed in the United States of America at Corporate Graphics in North Mankato, Minnesota.

TABLE OF CONTENTS

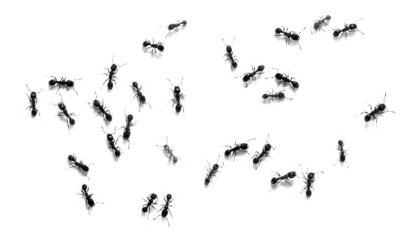

CHAPTER 1

MEET THE ANT!

Black eyes peer out from a hairy head. **Antennas** reach and feel. Strong, jagged jaws grab. What is this mighty **insect**? It is a tiny ant!

antenna

jaw

Around 10,000 ant **species** live on Earth. Some have big, strong jaws. Some have flat, round heads. All have the same three body parts. They are a head, a thorax, and an abdomen. Some have a stinger.

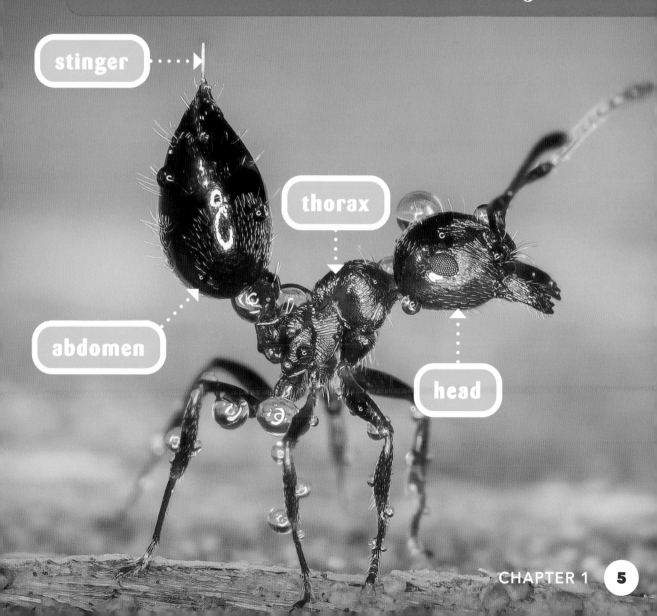

stinger

thorax

abdomen

head

All ants have six legs. Most adult ants can only walk. But some grow wings and fly, too.

wing

TAKE A LOOK!

Ants grow in four stages. Take a look!

1. Ants grow inside tiny eggs.

2. They hatch as **larvae**.

3. They form **cocoons** and change into **pupae**.

4. They become adults. Queens lay eggs.

To grow, ants need food. Some eat food made from animals and other insects. Aphids are insects that make **honeydew**. Ants drink the sweet liquid.

Ants eat insects, other ant eggs, and larvae, too. They also eat plants and **fungi**.

aphid

honeydew

When ants find food, they tell their **colony**. How? They leave a scent behind them. Other ants follow it to find the food.

DID YOU KNOW?

A mound ant can carry 5,000 times its weight. That is like a human lifting 11 semitrucks!

CHAPTER 2

WELCOME HOME

One by one, ants exit a sandy mound. They drop off clumps of dirt. What are they doing? They are building their home.

mound

egg

The mound leads to an underground nest. Tunnels connect many rooms. Some rooms hold eggs or larvae. Some store food. Some are for waste. One room is for the queen.

Different kinds of ants build their nests in different spaces. Carpenter ants dig in wood. They live in trees or in wooden buildings.

Weaver ants make nests from leaves. They use larvae silk to stitch leaves together.

DID YOU KNOW?

Ants nest in many different **habitats**. They live in rain forests and grasslands. They live in deserts and mountains, too. They do not live in cold places, such as Antarctica or Iceland.

carpenter ants

weaver ants

CHAPTER 3

ANT COLONIES

Ants live and work together in colonies. Some colonies have fewer than 100 ants. Others can have millions of ants!

Ants in a colony are different sizes. They have different jobs, too. Workers are small. They take care of the nest. Soldiers are bigger. They protect the nest. The queen is the largest. She lays eggs.

Soldier ants have a big job. They keep **predators** away. Spiders, snails, and birds attack. Anteaters lick a nest's tunnels.

But the strong soldiers know what to do. They bite with their big jaws. Some have poison or **acid**. They sting or spray their enemy. Others block the nest's entrance with their flat heads.

DID YOU KNOW?

Some ants die to protect the colony. How? They **flex** their bodies until they explode. A yellow poison shoots out.

young queen

When the weather gets warm, flying males and young queens leave their nests. They **mate**. Then, the males die.

New queens shed their wings. They find a new place to nest. Then, they lay eggs. The new ants are workers or soldiers. A new ant colony begins!

ACTIVITIES & TOOLS

CLOTHESPIN ANT MAGNET

Make an ant magnet in this fun activity!

What You Need:
- wooden clothespin
- black paint and paintbrush
- 2 black pipe cleaners
- scissors
- 3 black buttons
- glue
- 2 small googly eyes
- self-sticking magnet disc

❶ **Paint the clothespin black and wait for it to dry.**

❷ **Cut four two-inch (5-centimeter) pieces from the pipe cleaners.**

❸ **Glue three pieces of the pipe cleaner to the middle of one side of the clothespin. Center each pipe cleaner on the clothespin. These are the ant's legs.**

❹ **Now glue the three buttons on the clothespin. Put them over the legs. These are the ant's three main body parts.**

❺ **Bend the other piece of pipe cleaner. Glue it on top of the first button on the clothespin. These are the antennas on the ant's head.**

❻ **Glue the two googly eyes in front of the antennas.**

❼ **Peel the paper from the magnet disc. Stick it to the other side of the clothespin. Now you have an ant magnet!**

acid: A chemical substance that can dissolve some materials.

antennas: Feelers on the head of an insect.

cocoons: Coverings made by larvae or other small insects to protect themselves or their eggs.

colony: A large group of insects that lives together.

flex: To tighten a muscle or to bend or stretch.

fungi: Living things that are not animals or plants and may make mushrooms.

habitats: The places where animals or plants are usually found.

honeydew: A sweet liquid made by some insects.

insect: A small animal with three pairs of legs, one or two pairs of wings, and three main body parts.

larvae: Insects in the stage of growth between eggs and pupae.

mate: To come together to produce babies.

predators: Animals that hunt other animals for food.

pupae: Insects in the stage of growth between larvae and adults.

species: One of the groups into which similar animals and plants are divided.

INDEX

TO LEARN MORE

Finding more information is as easy as 1, 2, 3.

1. Go to www.factsurfer.com
2. Enter "ants" into the search box.
3. Choose your book to see a list of websites.

FACT SURFER